Remaining Calm in Troubling Times

Geary Reid

ISBN: 978-976-8305-27-5

Acknowledgements

Great thanks must be expressed to the following people:

The heavenly Father, for granting me the wisdom and inspiration to record the information in this book, which I began on April 24, 2021, and completed on May 3, 2021; my family, for their continued encouragement and support regarding various challenges; and several people who have assisted with reviewing and editing the book:

- Wonnette Nicholson, Dipl. in Business Management and Administration
- Judah Louisy, MSc, ACCA, FCPA

To you, the reader: have fun while reading, and grasp and practice what you learn so that this world will become a better place. Many people are depending on your guidance. We all need a shoulder to lean on and a hand to guide us.

Geary Reid
MBA, FCCA, FAAPM, MPM, CAT

Reid's Learning Institute and Business Consultancy

reidnlearn.com

Amazon: amazon.com/author/gearyreid

Facebook: Reid n Learn

Instagram: Reid n Learn

LinkedIn: Reid's Learning Institute
and Business Consultancy

199 Kuru - Kururu, Soesdyke Linden Highway
Guyana, South America

Table of Contents

Introduction

Problems are everywhere! No one can avoid all the problems that will cross their path.

When problems come, some persons lose their calm. Not everyone is able to remain calm when others try to hurt them. It appears to some persons that even when they seek to do well, troubles will still find them. Since no one can avoid all problems, then persons must find coping skills and remain calm, as some troubles will be over very soon. But if problems are ever-present, what must persons do to become victorious? This literature provides many solutions for how you can remain calm and have regular victories.

This literature is divided into five sections looking at the problems that persons face in different areas of their lives, and it also provides solutions to many of these problems.

Working persons face many problems. Sometimes, they even wish that they were not working, since they constantly have problems to address. Problems among employees can come from other coworkers or even supervisors. When some supervisors are having troubled days, they may unconsciously do things that cause other employees to be hurt. Some employees may hate a coworker and do things to cause them to fail. Nevertheless, with workplace problems, employees have to remain calm. If they choose not to remain calm, they may eventually have to look for other employers.

Not everyone owns their transportation. Those who have to travel on public transportation sometimes have to find ways to remain calm, as some passengers and drivers may do worrying things. If persons want to avoid traffic congestion, then they must leave their homes early to avoid problems with the traffic.

Every family has its issues. Some persons will do things to their family members that will cause them to become uncomfortable. If everyone tries to contribute positively within the family, then they can ease some of the tensions that family members go through.

Religious institutions are not free from problems. These problems are often created by people. However, some religious persons will seek to have peace with each other. Some followers may choose to pray so that peace will fill the hearts of everyone.

If many persons entertain positive thoughts, then they will leave little room for evil thoughts. Exercising can be another way of easing tension. Those who want to exercise can use some simple options and get great victories while releasing toxins from their systems. Building relationships is something that everyone must do, and those who are open to suggestions may find solutions to their problems.

1. Problems are inevitable

Problems do not have a birthday. Problems do not have a physical structure. Whenever a problem comes, it often changes many things. Some persons may have success after problems come, while others may regret the day that they were born or the day when problems visited them.

Problems will always be unwelcome guests whose impact can change the course of someone's life. Strong-willed persons will look for solutions whenever they face problems, while those who lack confidence will fall prey to problems.

Many persons will recognize that they seem to be unable to live a year without problems. They may also recognize that they can remember many problems in each month of their lives. Some may even experience problems weekly or daily.

Great planning is always good, but that does not stop problems from occurring. Problems are inevitable; they do not only occur because of a lack of sound planning. When a person dies, they will be free from problems, but their surviving relatives will still have problems to encounter. In some families, it appears that the death of one person opens more avenues for problems. For example, the death of a breadwinner can create problems for those who were depending on that person's income. In cases where the other companion was not working but depending upon the breadwinner, the surviving partner may eventually have to seek employment to generate enough money to take care of the family.

Many parents will constantly teach their children to do everything necessary to stay away from problems. However, despite the parents' best advice, some children will deviate from what they were taught. Within the minds of some children, they must experiment with some things, only to find themselves falling into the very problems of which they were forewarned. After one bad experience, some children learn their lessons and will not do certain things again. However, some children are like a magnet for problems, and they will explore many things, constantly getting themselves into more problems. Many caring parents will make attempts to help their children out of their problems.

Persons may attend work and plan to have a great day. They will manage their time and other resources before the working day is completed. However, before the workday is completed, they may have to address some problems. Not all employees will do the right things, and an error made by one employee may create problems for their coworkers.

Many drivers will use the roadway correctly. However, another driver's error, a pedestrian, or an animal may cause some drivers to encounter a problem they did not foresee.

Persons who have a good relationship with the Creator will often pray for themselves and others. They will often do things that will help others and encourage others to do the right things. However, sometimes, before they leave home or after they return home, they will encounter problems.

Some persons are very health conscious. They will ensure that they exercise regularly, consume a balanced diet, and visit medical practitioners. Nevertheless, despite all of these efforts, they may become ill. Sometimes, medical practitioners become ill with the same things they are specialists in.

Life is not free from problems until a person is dead. According to many religious teachings, even those who die will have to give answers for what they did when they were alive, and if they did bad things, then they will have to answer to the Creator.

Very few mothers will become pregnant and give birth and claim that they did not experience any problems, even if they followed all of the medical practitioners' advice and the advice of mothers who have given birth. When children are born, many persons speak of the joy those children will bring to the world, but sometimes those children contribute to many problems within their homes and societies.

Many vehicle manufactures will have quality control checks conducted on their vehicles before the vehicles are sold. Nevertheless, some vehicles will develop problems within months after they were purchased. Similarly, manufacturers of computers will work towards quality computers, but some customers will buy a computer and soon experience problems with it.

If problems were to be eliminated throughout the world, then some persons would be sad. Many businesses are established because needs exist or because there are problems to be fixed. One person's problem can lead to another person's opportunity.

Figure 1. How different persons consider problems

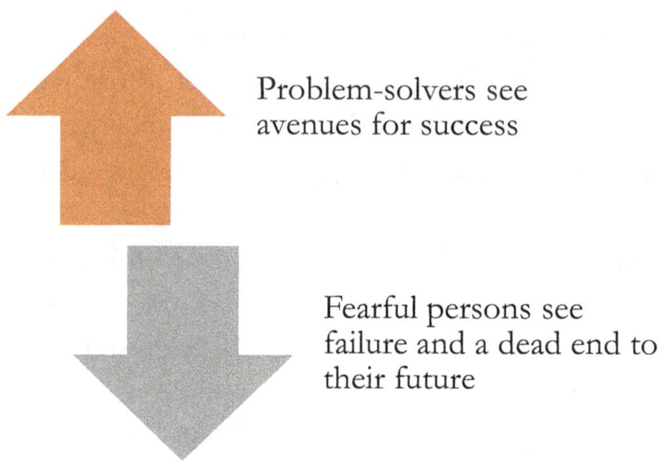

(All figures developed by the author unless otherwise noted.)

Sometimes, it is not the size of the problem that causes failure, but it is the size of the response that can contribute to the failure or success. Whenever problems appear, some persons think of all the things that can go wrong, without thinking about how many things can go right.

For those persons who hate mathematics, as soon as they see unfamiliar figures, they become uncomfortable. However, many mathematics teachers will tell students to put the figure into the formula and then solve the problem. That is what is often needed in life: to find a solution to a challenge, put that challenge into the formula and then get the possible outcome.

Those who have problems may attempt to run from them, but they will soon be visited by the same problems they ran from. Those who are not afraid of problems will look for solutions. Sometimes, persons have to stand up to their problems, find solutions, and conquer the problems.

2. Can you hide from problems?

Sometimes persons become tired of having to deal with problems, and they would like to have a vacation from their problems. If some persons could run away from problems, they would have done so. Problems are inevitable, and persons must find solutions if they want to survive.

Persons sometimes move away from one community with the intention that they will be free from some problems. However, shortly after they enter the new community, they encounter the same or similar problems once again.

Changing employment may make some persons feel that they will be free from all problems, but then they encounter similar problems in their new job. A similar thing happens where persons move to a new country, hoping that life will now bring them great and continuous success. No country is free from problems.

2.1 Problems above the earth

If a person were to take a flight and move beyond the earth's surface, then they would recognize that they still have problems to address. They may carry all of the food and water that they need. Nevertheless, they will not have all of the freedom to which they are accustomed. They may also recognize that they cannot move from one location to another location whenever they feel like it, incurring some cost.

If persons get close to the sun without any protection from it, they will soon recognize that the heat of the sun will make them uncomfortable. When persons go beyond the clouds, they cannot expect rain.

2.2 Problems on the earth

Living on earth has its challenges. Some persons hate insects and animals. However, these insects and animals were created for a purpose and are also important for human existence. If all insects and animals were to be removed from the earth, then human existence would be negatively affected.

In some countries, there are regular power outages. In other countries, while they have a stable supply of electricity, they have problems with droughts or too much rain. The humidity in some countries may make some persons uncomfortable. Some communities are easily affected by a flood, since they are in areas where water easily settles. The cost of living may be high in some countries, although those persons whose salaries are comfortable may not be seriously affected by the high cost of living.

2.3 Problems below the earth's crust

If persons could choose where they wanted to live, some of them may consider living below the earth's crust. But they have to consider that they can be affected by flooding, where excess water from the earth's surface may affect them. Those who live next to water tables may see excess water flowing into their space below the earth's crust.

Some plants may not be able to survive the heat generated when living below the earth's crust, and people will also be affected by it. There will be a low level of oxygen below the earth's crust, which makes it difficult to breathe.

Those who live on the surface of the earth will enjoy the sunlight whenever the sun is out. However, below the earth's crust, those who need light will have to use devices to provide it.

Section 1. Working persons

Persons who are working will face many problems, even those who are properly prepared for work.

All employees must know that even though they will face numerous problems, they must find ways to remain calm. Whenever employees do not address their problems, they can create more harm for themselves and others.

Those who are employed will be reporting to someone. Sometimes, while both of them intend to have a good conversation, something might be said or done that causes one person to become uneasy with the other. As mature employees, they must make every effort to prevent their situation from escalating and find ways to remain calm.

All employees must make it their practice to be at work on or before the required time. When employees are late, it causes customers to behave in unpleasant ways, and that can cause many distractions.

Each employee, whether junior or senior, must take responsibility for their actions. More employees must seek to remain calm, rather than creating problems for others.

3. Listening carefully to others

Many persons are employed because they have a passion for work. Persons also work because they have to provide for themselves and their families. Some persons work because they do not want to stay home.

However, whatever someone's reason for working, they must be willing to listen to others. Many persons can save themselves from certain problems if they will only listen to what others have to tell them. After some persons find themselves in trouble, they recognize that if they had listened to their workmates, they could have saved themselves from those problems.

3.1 Listen to lower-level employees

Some persons are not interested in taking advice from lower-level employees. They think that the lower-level employees cannot offer them any information that will help them. However, if a person wants to stay away from problems, then they must be willing to listen to employees of all levels.

Some employees are very caring. They look out for other employees and will often try to do things to protect them from problems. However, they are some lower-level employees who want their coworkers to fall into problems. They will do everything possible to cause other employees to have a negative report.

Table 1. Lower-level employees may be helpful with their conversation

Types of lower-level employees	Why they might be helpful with their conversation
Receptionists and telephone operators	Much information passes through them from both internal and external persons. They may sense danger from some conversations and may have inside information that can be used to avoid problems.
Gardeners	While gardeners will mainly be responsible for looking after the plants within the compound, they may also see and know some things that may be harmful if persons do them. If the compound is flooded, for example, gardeners may have information that they can share with those who may be involved in the construction

	or refurbishment of a building in the same compound.
Mechanics	Some organizations may employ mechanics. These individuals can provide good advice to users of company vehicles, which can save those employees from accidents.
Janitors	Too often, employees ignore janitors. However, when some senior officers are frustrated, they may share information with the janitors. With the information the janitors now have, they can help other employees to avoid many problems. Some janitors may be working for the same organization for several years and know some things that are right and wrong, which new employees may not be aware of.
Office Attendants/Assistants	Office attendants or office assistants often move among various managers and departments. They may hear of information that can be

	very helpful for many employees. Some of these office assistants or office attendants may also have access to external information as they interact with persons from various organizations.
Secretaries/Administrative Assistants	Many supervisors and managers should listen to their secretaries or administrative assistants. These individuals may have access to many correspondents, which may equip them with useful information to offer quality advice.

3.2 Listen to managers

Working persons must also listen to their supervisors and managers. Because of the supervisors' and managers' academics and experience, they may be able to provide quality advice to other employees. Many supervisors and managers will attend meetings that may provide them with a preview of useful information, which can enable many employees to avoid problems.

If employees want to remain calm, then they must be willing to stay away from problems. As those employees listen to the sound advice of their supervisors and managers, they may be better equipped to make decisions that will produce positive outcomes.

3.3 Listen to business owners

Many business owners have been in business for multiple years. They have seen many problems and have learned to remain calm. They also understand how to avoid certain problems. Therefore, employees must seek opportunities to learn from business owners and do the right things at the beginning. Some business owners are very caring for their employees and will treat them lovingly. Some employees can approach their business owners on almost any matter and get a proper answer.

Employees who want to remain calm must be willing to listen to many persons and take their positive advice. While persons have the opportunities to learn many things at school, they may learn some life skills from other employees that will be very useful in helping them to remain calm.

4. Attending work on time

When employees arrive at work after the established time, it sometimes leads management to have discussions with those employees. These discussions can be in the form of a mild conversation or a warning. With most organizations, a first-time offender may be given a verbal warning, but warning letters may have to be issued to those who are habitual latecomers.

Therefore, if an employee is looking forward to having a calm day at work, then that employee must arrive at work on time.

Figure 2. Importance of arriving at work before the required time

The employee can have a few minutes of relaxation

The employee has time to tidy up their working area

The employee is able to visit the restroom and return to the worksite before the required time

During performance appraisal or employee assessment, timekeeping will not be a matter of discussion for employees who attend work on time

The employee's salary does not have to be reduced because of late attendance

Many employees do not recognize that they sometimes cause their managers to become angry with them, especially when they come to work late. There are some situations where employees may be late to work, for example, in the case of traffic congestion or an emergency. However, employees must make it their practice to arrive at work at or before the required time.

Those employees who arrive at work before the start time may recognize that they have some time to relax and prepare themselves properly. When employees are rushing to get their work completed, they are more likely to make mistakes. Some of these mistakes can be very harmful to that employee or their coworkers. The danger that can be caused when employees are late for work can cause damage to the entire organization.

Every employee must be willing to make sacrifices to attend work on time. These sacrifices will often work in their favor. Employers love employees who take their timekeeping seriously and are willing to arrive at work before the start of their work hours.

Employees sometimes wonder why their managers have become angry with them, but they fail to recognize that because they attend work late, it causes the manager to become upset with their timekeeping. The undue pressure that the employee's lateness places the manager under causes the manager to become upset with other employees.

In some workplaces, employees are required to clean their work areas before they leave for the day. In other workplaces, employees are required to come to work early to keep their work area clean and to ensure that all the resources they need are available to them before they start their day of work.

If more employees make greater efforts to attend work on time, they will be doing something good for themselves. Some employees want their full pay but do not want to be at work on time. Employees want their managers to give them good reports at the end of the year, but they sometimes do not attend work on time. When employees respect their managers and the organizations and are doing the correct things, they can avoid any tension and have many great days at their workplaces.

5. Be productive and produce quality work

Many persons who are working must train themselves to produce quality work. Those persons who fail to do so will often be asked to redo the work, or someone may have to do the same work and complete it on the first attempt.

Too many persons wonder why their supervisor may be upset with them. However, those employees whose performance is unacceptable place themselves in positions where their work has to be constantly reviewed.

When supervisors are comfortable with their employees' work, they may spend less time reviewing all the details, since they have experience with quality work from those employees. When supervisors have to spend less time rechecking work, employees may have more time to perform their duties.

Employees who want to produce quality work must spend time learning what they have to do. They must also have a desire to produce quality work. When some persons start working, they may not know how to do everything yet, but it must be their intention to constantly increase their knowledge and skills. They can do this by attending learning institutions, learning from experienced employees, and engaging in trial and error. When employees master their skills, they become an asset to the organization, and many persons will enjoy working with them.

Incremental improvement must be something that every employee plans to do. They must understand that they will not know everything at the beginning, but they must constantly look for areas where they can improve.

Those persons who deliver quality work can obtain peace at their organization, since they are aware that their supervisor will often be satisfied with their work. Those who produce quality work must also complete their work on time. When the work is completed, then the relevant supervising officers must be informed on time.

Sometimes, when employees produce quality work, they provide themselves with opportunities to be considered for promotion. Most managers like to work with employees whose work meets the organization's expectations. Some managers will often seek employees who know their work, get their work done on time, and are respectful to other employees.

Employment options may be limited in some organizations. However, managers are often willing to concede to employees whose work is acceptable. Managers and supervisors are constantly looking for employees who can produce acceptable work. It costs the organization less money if employees can produce quality work at the beginning, so no cost has to be incurred to correct previous mistakes.

Section 2. Traveling

From time to time, persons will have to move from one location to another. Traveling can be an enjoyable thing for some persons. However, when some persons have to travel, they encounter many problems.

On some public transportation, the drivers will play songs that make the passengers relax. However, there are other drivers whose choice of songs makes the passengers uncomfortable throughout their journey and their week.

Some persons who use public transportation have a few drivers whom they will use frequently. These drivers understand their passengers and will often do things to make the passengers relaxed, which includes selecting songs that will motivate the passengers and driving within the speed limit.

Most persons who want to reach their destination on time must leave home early. Those who leave home early can avoid the rush hour traffic and probably avoid any potential accidents. Traveling on time requires some discipline from the driver and the passengers. Those persons who travel on time often have a calm day.

6. Listening to relaxing songs

When persons have to travel, there are many things that can be distracting. Not everyone can afford their own transportation. Therefore, they will have to use the public transportation system to move from one location to the other. Other persons are fortunate to have friends and family members who will transport them to many places.

Many persons will listen to relaxing songs while traveling. Those who have their own vehicles can play the music at the volume that is most comfortable for them. When the music is enjoyable, those who are playing the songs may sing along.

6.1 Select your songs

To be in a relaxing mood, persons should select the right songs. Not all songs will put persons in a relaxing mood. Some persons will not give much attention to certain songs. For each individual to be in a relaxing mood, their choice of a song may vary, yet they all may get the same outcome of feeling relaxed.

Persons with their own private vehicles can choose songs and play them over and over again. Those who play songs to help them relax may have favorite singers.

6.2 Select radio stations

Some radio stations consistently play songs that some persons embrace. These songs often place persons in a relaxing mood and cause them to accomplish many things. Many persons who have had to prepare for examinations might have listened to certain songs that helped them to concentrate on their studies.

When traveling in private transportation, persons may choose the songs that they want to listen to. Those who are traveling by public transportation may enjoy the songs that the driver selects. Some drivers of public transportation are very selective in their songs, based upon the passengers' age range, religious background, or culture. Some persons will only travel with specific drivers who select radio stations that cause the passengers to relax. They prefer to wait for these drivers or leave their homes early just to travel with them.

6.3 Relaxing songs are like medicine

Sometimes the challenges that persons go through mean that they need some songs to help them relax. Those songs operate like medicine for their minds. While they listen to those songs, the challenges they face will soon vanish.

Those who have many stressful things in their lives may choose songs that give them the courage to go through their day and allow them to be victorious. Not every day will be peaceful, and so persons may need something that gives them hope to enjoy life.

6.4 Songs via mobile devices

In recent decades, persons have the option to listen to songs while they exercise. Some persons listen to songs as they work in the office or in their yards. A caution to some persons: while listening to songs, be conscious of your environment and ensure that the volume is not so loud that it prevents you from being aware of any danger.

Many of these mobile devices give people opportunities to listen to songs as they study in the home, classrooms, or library. Persons who attend gyms may also have the opportunity to listen to music as they keep themselves fit.

7. Leave home on time

To remain calm, persons can also consider leaving home on time. Some persons think that they can get anywhere on time even when they leave home late, but leaving home on time is often important to do.

7.1 Avoid rush hour

In many countries, there is rush hour, which often causes persons to be late. Those who reach their destinations late are often confused and may be unsettled in their thinking.

For those persons who are employed, they may have to provide a reason why they are late to work. In cases where customers are waiting for employees to get to work at a specific time, there can be some uneasiness with those customers. In some communities and countries, customers have the option to choose the same product or service from different organizations. Therefore, no one organization has a monopoly over the customers.

During rush hour, many drivers will make all attempts to avoid accidents. However, not all drivers will operate as defensive drivers, and there may be an accident. Every accident, whether small or large, will have a cost attached to it.

Insurance companies are willing and prepared to settle some accidents, but the vehicle must first be insured. The type of vehicle insurance will also determine whether either driver can receive any benefits. If the cost of the accident is minor, the owner of the vehicle may have to pay the full cost, since the cost of the accident does not surpass the excess ceiling.

Persons who are traveling to important events or from one country to another must also be aware of their time and avoid the rush hour. Some persons have missed their flight because they did not manage their time. Many times, for persons who have to travel through several countries and airports for interconnected flights, missing a flight may cause major rescheduling. There may also be a cost attached to obtain another flight to their intended destination.

Missing a meeting because of rush hour delay may cause some persons to miss business opportunities. Not all business opportunities can be deferred.

7.2 Avoid congested places

Sometimes, it may be very difficult to find important places where there are only a few customers there. However, if some persons leave home early, they may be able to avoid the congestion.

In some communities, there may be alternative places that may not be as popular but offer the same product. On some occasions, there may be a slight price difference, but it may be most appropriate to pay a few dollars more and avoid waiting for a long period.

When some places are congested, customers can behave in an unruly manner, and that may cause persons to engage in unnecessary conversation and confrontation. Therefore, those persons who leave home early can avoid congested places or choose alternative places to obtain the same goods and services.

7.3 Plan to leave home early

To reach many places on time requires some planning. Before a person leaves their home or workplace, they have certain things to do. With knowledge of what they have to do, they must also manage their time for various activities, some of which will consume a lot of time. Those activities which cannot be completed within the same day will have to be completed in the next day or at another appropriate time.

When persons fail to make plans, they often become overwhelmed with the activities ahead of them and the little time available to perform them. Planning one's time is very important for every individual, especially if they want to complete certain things promptly.

Time has never promised to wait for anyone, no matter the status of that person. Therefore, everyone must be conscious that time is always moving away from them, and they must do whatever is necessary to use the time available to them to get the results they need.

Persons who want to reach a place on time must be willing to leave their home on time. This will require that they be disciplined with their time management so that they do not become frustrated because of their poor time management.

Section 3. Within your family

Family members must try to have peace with each other. Each family member needs the others.

In some families, if each family member contributes to the household activities, then there will be peace within the family. While everyone wants to have a clean house and have food on the table, they must be prepared to make their own contributions.

Families may have their conflicts, as each person has their own value systems. However, family members must seek to resolve their problems as they live as one.

When family members are having problems, they often need someone to assist them. Within some families, there may be one or two family members who are motivators to the others. Those who need help can go to them for assistance.

For those family members who need help, they must show an interest and be respectful in asking for help. When persons need help, they must be willing to work with the guidance of those persons who can help them.

8. Be helpful

The tasks that have to be done within any home are many. While some persons within the home may take great responsibility to perform certain tasks, many more members ought to provide some assistance. If persons take some time and consider, they will understand that everyone within the home benefits from that which is done within the home.

In some homes, there is confusion and regular arguments because certain members within the home feel that they do not have to make any contribution. Some persons like to enjoy the work done by others without giving their support.

Once there are more hands and minds to do the same thing, then more can be accomplished. When more is accomplished, there is less time for conflicts and more time for meaningful conversation.

8.1 Develop your skills within the home

No one is born knowing to do all the right things. Therefore, they need to spend some time learning. Some domestic activities are best learned within the home, rather than in the classroom.

Many parents are delighted when their children learn some essential skills from the home. These essential skills will be beneficial not only now but also for their future. Many children, when they become adults, will have their own families. The skills children learn with their parents will be important for them to demonstrate within their new families.

Learning to do many different things within the home is very good. While some persons may have a specific task they prefer to do within the home, they must learn to do many different things. Every essential skill learned will be very helpful whenever persons are living alone or with their new families. In cases where some family members have to travel to a different country for work or study, they may have to exercise the skills they learned at home.

8.2 More hands

Family household activities are many and can be overwhelming. Family members who are at home full time can feel burdened by having to perform many family duties. Therefore, if other members of the family make their own contributions, they will ease some tension within the home. Those who were once stressed out will have reasons to celebrate and remain calm as other family members have assisted in completing the work.

In the beginning, some family members will make mistakes. However, with constant practice, they are expected to improve their skills. With improved skills, more is done, and fewer things have to be corrected.

8.3 No gender bias

Parents must remind their children that many of the tasks which have to be performed within the home are not gender biased. In some communities and families, some persons believe that certain tasks are assigned to a particular gender. But when many persons choose to get more work done within the home without considering gender, every member of the family will have more time to enjoy each other's friendship.

Both boys and girls must learn to do many things within the home. Males and females must not stereotype certain tasks within the home, but be willing to do whatever needs to be done, since the entire family will benefit from their contributions.

9. Connect with positive family members

Within some homes, certain family members are great influencers. These are persons with whom other family members often connect because they can make others feel comfortable and motivated.

These positive family members often have hearts to help other persons. They may even leave themselves undone just to help others.

A simple discussion with positive family members can make some persons energized to conquer many things that once seemed impossible. Sometimes, without much being said, just being around family members who have a positive outlook on life may be adequate to stir other persons to do good things or to cause them to remain calm.

Life often has many challenges. Some of these challenges may cause persons to want to give up, but with some positive-thinking family members, there is hope for other family members to feel great about their future.

9.1 Be willing to learn

Those persons who want to remain calm among positive-thinking family members must be willing to learn. Too many persons do things to impress others. However, it is often good to spend time learning from others who know more or who are willing to influence others to do the right things.

Learning can be very challenging for some persons. However, everyone should adopt an attitude of wanting to learn. Not everyone will be able to positively influence others, but those who can influence others find joy in making them feel great.

There are not many persons who want to pour their positive energy into others to make them feel great. Therefore, individuals who have such persons in their family must complement those family members.

9.2 Be willing to share

There are many challenges in life. However, family members who are willing to positively influence others can make a great difference in their family as they share their knowledge and experiences.

When persons are going through challenges, they must be willing to share their concerns. As they share their concerns, other family members may be willing to assist them. Sometimes, persons go through many challenges alone, without getting much assistance. This happens because they refuse to seek help. No one has all the answers to every problem. However, those who share their concerns may find other family members who can share how they have overcome certain challenges.

9.3 Select positive family members to emulate

Not every family member may be good to emulate. However, some family members can add great value to the lives of others. These family members are like role models. They are willing to see other persons grow and be not offended.

Whenever there are positive role models within the family, others need to congratulate them and let them know that they are doing a good job. For those persons who want to remain calm and find a positive role model within their family, they must be willing to spend some time learning from them. While the process of learning can be lengthy, both persons must be willing to work with each other.

Learning from positive-thinking people may be costly, but the rewards can be great. It is very difficult to place a price on persons having peace within themselves and remaining calm. Many persons know the amount of money they spend when they visit medical practitioners for stress and health-related issues. It is better to stay healthy and remain calm, which allows a person to live many years.

Section 4. Religious institutions

Those who embrace religion have often seen that whenever they are having difficult days, they can seek divine help. Some persons will worship or pray so that they will have a calm day.

Within many religious institutions, there are teachings for the followers that guide them in remaining calm in troubling times. Even religious leaders and followers will have troubling times, but when they seek the help of the Creator, they often have a blessed season.

Remaining calm is not always about human strength or intelligence. Those who embrace religion know that they are successful today because of the divine assistance they have received, especially when they were faced with troubling times.

10. Study religious teachings

Many persons have, or once had, a religious background. These religious backgrounds have provided them with many answers to their concerns.

10.1 Why study religious teachings?

Some persons spend many hours studying religious literature every week or month. Those who are devoted to their faith will constantly keep increasing their knowledge.

Figure 3. Reasons why persons study religious teachings

They become more aware of their religion

They are better able to defend their religion

They are better able to teach other persons about their religion

Family members may need answers to religious and social issues

> Religious teaching provides an understanding of what happens after physical death

> Religious learning provides peace to many persons

> Religious teaching helps many persons to stay away from problems

> Religious teaching helps many persons to enjoy their family and work lives

Some parents insist that their children become aware of the same religion their parents embrace. Therefore, these children will attend religious events with their parents. Beyond just attending religious events, some children will participate in these events and go on to occupy leadership positions.

Many children and adults have enjoyed calm in their lives because of their religious knowledge. Many persons may want to distract others, but those who learn about their religion and embrace those teachings will often allow troubling times to pass, as they know that better days are ahead of them.

Persons who attend religious teaching often try to be peacemakers. These individuals will choose peaceful ways of life and try to remain calm, even when many people and things around them are contributing negative energies.

Some religious leaders will constantly teach their followers to be positive role models. These religious leaders will ask certain followers to share some of their good experiences about how they have overcome many challenges. When persons share their positive experiences, those who listen to them are encouraged and want to remain committed to the religious institutions.

10.2 When to study religious teaching

Those who are committed to their religion will allocate some time for regular studies. They do so as often as possible, since they want to follow what is recorded in those religious books.

To be a good student of a particular religion, followers have to spend time learning. The more persons learn about their religion, the more joy they have in knowing what to do and how to help others.

Persons are free to choose times for religious learning that are most convenient for them. Some persons will establish a specific time to learn more about their religion, since they want to be good representatives of their religion.

10.3 Practice your religion

Besides attending religious institutions and reading religious literature, all followers need to practice what they have learned. Some persons will only follow a religion when they see other followers practicing what they have learned.

For persons to become effective in their religion, they have to practice what they have learned and be good examples to others. They must also maintain peace, respect others, and live well with people. This does not mean that they are excluded from life's challenges, but that they choose to do well, even when bad things are said about them or done to them.

Whenever persons are tested, they ought to demonstrate what they have learned. While some persons who are affiliated with a religion may feel that they should be exempted from some of life's challenges, they all have to face them. However, if they remain calm and have victories in many areas, they may become inspirations to many persons.

11. Participate in worship and prayer

Prayer is an essential part of some persons' lives. They do not leave their homes unless they pray. They will not eat their food unless they pray. If a new employment opportunity is available, they will pray before they make a decision. These individuals are committed to prayer as they need divine guidance in whatever actions and decisions they will make.

Each individual will worship the Creator in the ways they have learned and probably in ways that feel most comfortable to them. Some persons worship as they sense they have peace throughout their day. They understand that when they invite the Creator to be a part of their lives, their lives will remain calm.

11.1 Why pray regularly?

Many persons have proven that when they pray regularly, their days are blessed. Many problems that others encounter may not befall those who pray, since they sought divine protection.

Prayer must not be done only when persons have nothing else to do, and those who have a relationship with the Creator will see it as something that must be done regularly. In some religions, there are specific times during the day when followers are expected to pray. As they set aside time to pray, they feel energized and protected to continue the rest of their day.

As persons pray regularly, they must remember to pray for others. Their prayers must not be selfish, as they need the Creator to cause many persons to have a calm day or to accomplish many good things.

Parents will sometimes teach their children to pray. Therefore, when these children become adults, they see the need to pray regularly and may also teach their own offspring to do so.

Those who are working must remember to pray for their workmates. Some of the problems working persons encounter come from their workmates. Therefore, if prayers are said regularly for these workmates, then most of the days will be calm and many good things will be accomplished.

In most religions, the leaders will remind their followers to pray regularly. Members will pray when they attend a corporate gathering for the followers, and they will also pray when they are alone or with their families.

Prayers must also be extended for other nations. While some nations are going through their own problems, they may not find enough courage to pray and may need other persons to pray for them until they recover.

11.2 Why worship regularly?

Each individual may choose how often they want to worship the Creator. However, most religious persons will make it their practice to worship daily, weekly, monthly, etc., since they believe that the success they have is a result of the Creator's blessings on their lives.

Being thankful is something that many persons must do regularly. While some persons may not have all that they want, they may still proceed and give thanks. As they give thanks in advance, they often receive that which they are praying for.

Worshipping helps to strengthen the relationship of an individual with their Creator. Some persons have become dependent on a musical instrument in their worship of the Creator, but worship is beyond external things. Musical instruments can be used as support for worship, but persons must be taught that they can worship the Creator without a musical instrument.

11.3 Engage in private worship and prayer

When persons visit their main place of worship, they engage in corporate worship and prayer. Nevertheless, each individual must also have their own time of private prayer and worship. Prayer and worship must not be used to entertain persons or to showcase one's superior spiritual relationship. Rather, each person ought to find some private time to pray and worship the Creator.

Those who are comfortable with private worship and prayer may be courageous enough to worship and pray in public, but not everyone is bold enough. It is not where a person prays or worships that makes the difference. Many times, the prayers said by those who pray in private have a great impact.

When some persons worship in their private places, they have a calmness in their hearts. As they go through the day, they do not allow others to disturb them. The worship they engage in creates an atmosphere that gives them the joy to go through each day and expect that great things will follow them.

Section 5. Personal positive responses to remain calm

Each individual must be intentional about wanting to remain calm. They must make it their duty to remain calm despite everything that is happening. Too many persons are dying from stress-related problems, and many of the problems people have to deal with can be avoided or reduced.

One reason some persons get themselves in trouble is that they say too much without giving enough thought towards what they will say. When persons say less and think more, they can avoid some of the problems that are caused when persons are uninformed but choose to speak.

Everyone needs friends. However, they must choose to build good friendships. It is through these friendships that many persons find answers to their problems.

Those persons who are open to ideas and suggestions will give themselves opportunities to overcome their problems. Many persons have positive information and ideas, which will be useful for those who are facing problems. Not everyone has to go through all of the challenges in life to find solutions.

Every storm has a beginning and an end. While no one knows when the end of a storm will come, they must be confident that if they can remain calm during the time of the storm, they may soon have victories. When storms come, they make persons stronger and allow them to be overcomers.

12. Think much and say less

The reason some persons get themselves into problems is that they speak too much. While it is important to speak, some persons must think much and say less. Whether some persons say something or nothing, people will talk. However, it is important not to contribute fuel to their fire.

12.1 Give more thought towards thinking

Too many persons rush to speak. They believe that they will make great things happen whenever they speak. However, some persons need to spend more time gathering truth first.

There is great access to information, but some persons refuse to research the truth. Whenever persons gather the truth, they must then spend some time pondering on it.

Parents may remind their children to stay quiet. It is not that they do not want to hear from their children, but they know that their children did not give much time towards thinking about some matters before speaking.

12.2 Choose what to say

A good approach to staying out of problems is to choose what to say. While persons are expected to communicate, if they have to speak, they must manage the words they speak.

After a person has spoken, they cannot cancel what was said. Many times, people get into arguments because of what they have said. Even though some persons will apologize for what they said, they are unable to change what the other person heard.

While words do not have any physical form, they may be more powerful than many persons think. Nations go to war because of what someone says. Marital relationships are sometimes hurt because one partner did not choose the correct words.

Some persons perceive many things, and some of these perceptions have no merit. It is important to choose what to say and not to give persons ammunition with your words.

12.3 Choose when to speak

When persons make a deliberate effort to choose what to say, they must also choose when to speak. Another reason why some persons get themselves into problems with their communication is that they say something at the wrong time. Timing is critical when making a statement to someone.

For example, if a person is tired or angry, then it will be better not to engage them in certain conversations that will not help their present situation. While they may need to hear certain things, it may be better to tell them the same thing at a later time.

In the office, some supervisors and managers need to assess their staff regularly. Some employees are not easily disturbed when certain things are said to them, even when they are having a troubling day. However, other staff members cannot hear certain unpleasant conversations when they are experiencing a troubling day.

Parents must often assess their children's moods before communicating certain information with them. Children are not always having a good day, and any unpleasant information can make their day even more uncomfortable.

13. Exercising

Exercising must never be seen as a burden to the body, but an effort to enhance longevity and mental awareness. Persons are sometimes stressed out because they have not exercised. They have not allowed their minds and bodies to remove some unnecessary materials.

Everyone who wants to be in good health should make an effort to exercise. As they exercise, they are doing themselves a favor.

13.1 Exercising can reduce medical bills

If a person has not done regular exercises for some time, then they should begin doing so gradually. Indeed, starting to exercise again may be challenging for those who once were engaged in regular exercise. However, to restart exercising is a good decision, since many good things will happen for those who choose to exercise.

The medical bills some persons have to pay could have been avoided if they chose to exercise. Persons must typically visit their medical practitioners at least once a year. However, they must not wait for the medical practitioner to remind them of some of the basic things they must do.

If a person chooses to exercise, then they may not be incurring any major cost, but rather reducing the possibility of having to pay high medical bills. These exercises do not strain their body, but just help to keep them fit and alert.

13.2 Basic exercise

Some persons want to engage in exercise but may not have the time to do so. Others may think that they have to get special clothes or attend a gym to exercise.

However, there are some basic exercises that many persons can be engaged in. These exercises can be done within a person's personal space and time. Even those who are employed can exercise without having to leave the office.

Figure 4. Basic exercise

Basic exercise at home	Basic exercise at work
☐ Clean the yard	☐ Move around the office and avoid telephone calls to people nearby
☐ Wash the vehicle or house	☐ Assist others who may not be able to move around at a particular moment
☐ Cook and do laundry	☐ Park farther away and walk to your destination
☐ Establish a kitchen garden, if there is enough space and the weather and soil are adequate	☐ During your lunch break, engage in activities that will help you to exercise

Some of these exercises are so basic that anyone might be able to do them. It is expected that many persons will make a deliberate effort to exercise, as they reduce their potential medical bills and enhance their longevity.

13.3 Reducing stress

Many persons are affected by stress. Sometimes they are stressed about things they have no control over. Some persons are stressed because of work or economic situations. Parents can also be very stressed because of their children's actions and behaviors.

However, when persons exercise, they have opportunities to redirect their energies in doing something that will take their minds away from those things that are causing stress. When some persons are stressed, they can become very violent, but as they put more energy towards their exercise, they may soon recognize that whatever was affecting them mentally has subsided or disappeared.

Some organizations have equipment for employees to exercise. These employees can exercise at times that are most convenient to them but without affecting their production for the organization. After they finish exercising and go home, have their dinner, take some rest, and return to work for the next day, they feel much relief.

Some gyms provide punching bags, which serve many purposes to many persons. Besides using them to develop strength in their arms, some persons take out their anger on the punching bags. So, for example, if a supervisor has caused an employee to become angry, the employee can hit the punching bag with as much energy as they need to relieve their frustration.

13.4 Regular walking

Those who do not get to walk regularly should consider doing so. It may not have to be for long distances. However, some amount of walking is very good for anyone who can stand on their feet.

In some communities, friends, families, and workmates may walk together. As they walk, they can discuss many matters. Sometimes they can talk about marital issues. Parents can talk about similar concerns they are experiencing with their children and discuss possible solutions.

Many persons choose to walk in national or local parks. Many of these parks have safe spaces for persons to walk and to stop and talk. Both young and elderly persons can use these parks to exercise. There may be a small fee to enter some parks, but it may be a worthwhile investment. In many government-owned parks, there may not be any cost to enter.

Those who use the parks must observe the rules. Persons must not litter within the park; instead, they must use any garbage receptacles that are available to them.

Those who choose walking as a form of exercise must know that they are not in a competition, but they are doing something that will cause them to remain calm and find solutions to their problems. As some persons walk, they recognize that they have solutions to their problems. When they finish their walking exercise, they are rich with ideas and are ready to address many of the problems that once confronted them.

13.5 Healthy diet

Keeping a healthy body is important for those who want to exercise. However, it must be every person's intention to be healthy.

To become healthy, some persons may have to manage what they consume. While exercising is good, persons must be intentional in what they eat and drink. To reduce medical bills, persons must have a balanced diet. Too many persons are not enjoying their senior years because they did not choose to eat and drink healthy things when they were younger.

Today is a good day to start eating and drinking healthy products. Consider the information in the table below and manage what you eat and drink from this day onwards.

Table 2. The five main groups of nutrients

Main groups of nutrients	Explanation	Sources of the nutrients
Protein	The primary function of protein is to provide bodybuilding or growth materials, so every cell in the body contains proteins.	Meat, fish, cheese, eggs, wheat, rice, oats, beans
Fat (and oil)	Provides a convenient and concentrated source of energy, supplying more energy than the same weight of	Meat, butter, margarine, fish, nuts, fruits

	carbohydrate or protein.	
Carbohydrates	Carbohydrates are the most important source of energy for the body. Almost all the cells of the body use glucose to distribute energy. Carbohydrate acts as a "protein sparer" so that protein can be used for its primary functions rather than as a source of energy.	Sugar, honey, molasses, jam, jelly, yam, sweet potato, breadfruit, rice, barley, corn
Vitamins	Vitamins are a group of chemical substances, most of which were identified during the 20th century as vital to the body. The body requires only small amounts of each vitamin. Vitamins can be	Milk, cheese, eggs, carrot, spinach, watercress, cabbage, tomato, pumpkin, Callaloo, cod liver oil

	classified according to the substances in which they dissolve.	
Minerals	Bodybuilding. Control of bodily processes. Essential parts of body fluid. Some mineral elements are required in relatively large amounts.	Milk, cheese, broccoli, bok choy, legumes, bread

(Extract from Tull and Coward, 2009)

14. Build good friendships

When persons are hurt by the actions of others, they sometimes do not want to open themselves to establishing a friendship with other persons. However, they must not expect the bad experience with one person to happen again with others. Life has many opportunities and many good people. Some good persons are interested in helping other persons to find solutions to their problems. They may be willing to build a friendship with others so that they can experience the goodness of life.

There are many hurting people, and there are many who are having great days. Those who are hurting must assess if they are causing harm to themselves and what actions they must take. Each person needs friends regardless of their status and age. Some friends may have their own intentions and look out for their interests alone, so it is important to have some friends who have a genuine concern to help others.

14.1 Recognize that there is a need for friendship

Unless a person recognizes that they need friends, they will not make themselves available to become friends with others. There are some introverts who prefer to be alone as much as possible. Some persons will try to avoid letting others get close to them, since they do not want to be friends with others.

On the other side, some persons need many friends. They will make a great effort to connect with persons to become their friends.

When a person recognizes that they need friends, then they must be open enough to allow persons to come into their space. They must also be willing to go after persons who can be there for them. To remain calm in troubling times, people need friends who will be there for them and provide support during the challenging moments of life.

14.2 Identify possible persons to become your friends

Not everyone is a good friend. Some persons' intention in any friendship is to see how others will provide for them. Other persons want all the attention to be given to them whenever they become friends with others.

It is important to identify persons who will respect and support you. Too many persons only want to become friends with others for the things they can get. As soon as they are unable to receive the things they need, then the friendship is over.

When building a friendship that will help you to remain calm, take some time to learn about the person's background. Many persons are good at pretending that they are good friends, but later they will show that they were not a true friend.

As you build friendships, you are expected to share some important information about yourself. Not all friends are good enough to keep important information with them, since some of them are like spray cans, giving away all the material placed in them. Never underestimate the positive impact some friendships can produce. Therefore, it is important that, when choosing friends, you take time to identify a few genuine persons who are willing to be there for you.

14.3 Nurture your friendship

Friendship does not grow in isolation, nor without human intervention. Therefore, anyone who wants to have friends must be willing to invest in the other person. Some of the investments may not have any major costs associated with them. Sometimes, a telephone call once in a while may be important for both persons to do, or perhaps organizing a lunch date. Remembering your friends' birthdays and other anniversaries and communicating with them on those days may be very important to help the friendship to grow.

Other friendships may require more effort. For example, if one person is studying and depends on a friend to assist them with their schoolwork, this friendship may require both persons to talk with each other frequently.

Each friendship requires different levels of investment. Those who want the benefits of the friendship must be willing to invest in it, as both parties will grow together.

Because of the good friendships many persons have, they can find solutions to many of their problems. They can remain calm when trouble faces them, as they have strong friendships that provide answers to their challenges.

15. Be open to suggestions and ideas

No one has all the knowledge and ideas they need, so they need to be open to the views of others. Within many organizations, persons may work in groups or pairs. Some persons may have someone who supervises them. While some of these approaches are intended to enhance internal controls, they are also there to help others to share ideas.

The wisdom of one person may be limited. However, when several people team up, they get more done, as each person can bring their ideas to the discussions.

15.1 Show interest in learning

Persons can place a blockage on their learning by showing little regard for the ideas shared by others. Some persons refuse good information shared by others because they believe that their own ideas are always superior.

If some persons recognize that an individual is open to suggestions and wants to learn, then more information will be shared with them. When some persons are going through troubles, they feel that no one cares about them. However, they have shut their doors to receiving good information.

The problems some persons go through could have been avoided if they made themselves available to learn from others.

At some workplaces, some employees have not built friendships, nor have they shown that they want anyone to help them.

15.2 Ask for help

Help is often available, but some persons allow pride to fill their hearts and do not ask for help. Those who ask for help will receive ideas and suggestions from others. There are many solutions, but some of them will only become available to those who will ask for help.

Those who believe in the Creator know that if they need help, they must ask the Creator for help. While the Creator knows their need, they are still expected to seek help. This is also true for getting help from other people: those who need help must ask for help.

When countries are in crisis, they may seek help from other countries. When they ask for help, it does not mean that they are weak. Too many persons feel that if they seek help, then others will perceive them as inferior. However, even the strongest person or company needs help.

Those persons who belong to professional organizations or academic bodies know that they have that reservoir of persons from whom they can seek help. All they need to do is show their interest in being helped by others. Some of the help provided by academic bodies is free to their current and former students.

15.3 Align with learning institutions and people

Those who want to increase their ideas must be willing to align themselves with people who can share ideas with them, which can take place through learning institutions. Some persons may find answers to their problems through learning institutions.

Through the knowledge gained at learning institutions, many persons are able to improve.

16. Entertain positive thoughts

The human mind was never designed for evil and negative thoughts. Therefore, whenever a person is thinking evil, they must seek to cleanse their mind from such thoughts. The longer persons harbor evil thoughts in their minds, the more evil will flow through their mouths and the more they will do evil things.

16.1 Why consider positive thoughts?

There will be many distractions every day. Some distractions are caused by people's negative attitudes. There are other times when distractions happen because there are persons who hate to see others succeed.

Negative thoughts will never allow a person to become successful. When persons spend much energy and time thinking negatively, they are only hurting themselves.

Persons who consider positive thoughts give themselves many opportunities to become successful and to help others to become successful. In life, the actions of one person have a chain reaction on others. Therefore, when a person thinks and operates positively, they help other persons to realize their dreams.

16.2 How often to consider positive thoughts

Positive thoughts must not be a one-time event. Those who want to avoid problems and remain calm must allocate much of their time towards positive thinking. It must become their culture to give greater time for positive thoughts.

Many children follow the examples of their parents, so when parents begin to think positive thoughts, it can cause their children to follow a similar pattern. If more persons are going to walk away from problems and remain calm, then parents and other adults within the home must think and operate positively.

The earlier children can adopt an approach of thinking positively, the earlier they are giving themselves opportunities to become successful. Negative thoughts allow persons to see themselves as defeated. However, those who think positively will see themselves as victorious.

16.3 Ways to entertain positive thoughts

Listening to positive-thinking persons is one way to entertain positive thoughts. Those who like music may choose songs that will motivate them and put them in a positive mood. Some days can be very depressing, but with uplifting songs, some persons are motivated to make their day great. Those who listen to motivating songs and news may be able to take on many challenges in life and know that they have the ability to overcome those challenges.

Some persons will start their day with devotion and prayer. While doing this, they try to inculcate positive thoughts. After they have devotions, they are ready to face whatever challenges life will offer them, as they know that they have already enriched their spirits for the day.

17. The storm will be over

For everyone who is going through a storm, rest assured that the storm will be over. No storm is destined to stay forever. However, those who are prepared for the storm will be able to endure it, since they know that the storm will end and they will continue to accomplish what they set their minds to do.

In many boxing matches, one person will have an advantage over their opponent. They sometimes believe that they will bring the fight to an end very soon by landing a Technical Knock Out (TKO) against their opponent. However, the opponent may allow their challenger to become tired, and then when such time has come, the opponent begins to throw punches that may appear to be simple, but can be damaging enough to result in a TKO. However, what is important is to never give up when many problems confront you.

Those persons who have great success now will indicate that they went through many challenges. On many occasions, they thought of giving up, but they decided against it. Those who give up may have been near to their victory. Sometimes, it is important to change strategy to win the battle.

17.1 Stay committed

When persons stay committed, they allow themselves to become victorious. This commitment must be an inward thought, which will be manifested in the actions of the individual. It may take much energy to stay committed, but it is a good decision to make, as it allows a person to think of victory even when defeat is almost present.

Few persons will remain committed throughout many storms. Many persons give up early and live to regret it. Those who are committed often have testimonies of how they have overcome.

For those persons who have to prepare for an examination, they know that they have to study. Sometimes, during their studies, they face many obstacles, which will cause some of them to give up. However, other persons see these obstacles as opportunities for them. Those persons who have gone through similar storms are confident that life will not always be challenging to them, so they remind themselves that there is a victory for them in the future.

Persons who build good friendships may have the support of other persons as they go through their storms, who will be there to cheer them on and to remind them not to give up. Some of those support persons may also share their testimonies of how they were victorious after their own storms.

No one is free from going through a stormy period in their life. However, those who are committed will allow the storm to pass them by as they await the brighter days of life.

Many persons must remain calm during their storms, as those storms will one day be over. While there may be damage after the storm passes, there is still positive life after the storm.

18. Expect a great future

No matter what problems you are facing, expect a great future. Many people lose hope when they go through a difficult situation. However, difficult situations can often become a platform for greatness. Those who can overcome the storms must expect that great things will happen to them.

While there are many problems, those problems will not remain forever. So, expect that a new day will dawn upon your life.

18.1 Live for the future

Many persons only think of today, failing to think that better days will come. While some persons are having success today, they can have greater success in the future if they only plan big.

There will always be obstacles in life. However, some of the obstacles that are present today are actually a platform for greatness. When some students fail their examinations, they feel that life is over. However, as they study and sit the same examination again, they will recognize that their performance showed great improvement. During the preparation the second time, the student better understands many theories and concepts that they did not understand before, and they can easily apply those concepts and theories.

As persons think of the future, it sets their minds at ease that once they can go through the present problems, then they will have victory for the next day. Parents will often remind their children to remain focused and not to give up hope. These reminders have helped many children to look for brighter days, and indeed, many children have seen these brighter days unfold in their lives.

Even within some countries, there may be economic and political situations that make many residents uncomfortable. However, once persons vote for a change to a new political party, they may experience many good things.

Some upcoming athletes are disappointed when they fail. However, they must remain calm and continue to increase their skills. With constant improvements and continuing to enter the competitions, then one day, they may be declared the winner.

If farmers were to give up on the first occasion when their farm did not yield the success they so desired, then they probably all would have quit farming. However, every farmer must remember that if there is a failure in one season, they must remain calm and expect to have great victories in the next season.

When fishermen go to the sea to catch fish, they may not always get the catch they anticipate. However, as they return to the sea over and over again, they will be sounding the alarm of victory.

Too many persons give up after their first or second failures. However, they must anticipate that great days will become available to them in the future. Those who choose not to quit may be singing victory for many days hereafter.

Reference list

Tull, Anita, and Antonia Coward. 2009. *Caribbean Food and Nutrition for CSEC*. Oxford, UK: Oxford University Press.

About the Author

During his years of schooling, author Geary Reid made great attempts to avoid trouble. He often assesses situations, and if he senses that there may be trouble, he looks for peaceful solutions. When he visits his children at school, if he sees children arguing or fighting, he often tries to bring peace among them.

Even as a leader involved in religious activities, he often encourages others to remain calm. He encourages persons to carefully listen to each perspective before responding. He has seen too many persons get into arguments because of their choice of words or saying something at the wrong time.

Remaining calm takes much effort, and Geary Reid wants many persons to remain calm rather than cause problems. Oftentimes, it is easy for problems to come but difficult for them to leave.

Reid has seen many troubling times. He has seen how many persons struggle to remain calm when they are wrongfully accused. Distraction will visit everyone. Even great leaders have experienced many troubles, but because they have to remain calm and find strategies, they have now overcome. Since many persons have already overcome, Reid wants to help many other persons to become victorious.

Geary Reid has worked with both public and private sector organizations. He has had to meet many deadlines. He has met many employees who are angry and want other persons to become angry just like them. When some persons cannot get others to be on their side to create harm, they will work through different persons to share false information. Some managers would also like to see their subordinates fail.

Politicians may have their selected group of people, and they will do everything necessary to help their supporters, while the non-supporters of the government are often ostracized. However, those who remain calm will soon have their victories.

For some persons, remaining calm will take much effort. However, Reid provides many simple and practical ways to remain calm. If more persons remain calm, then they will be able to accomplish many great things.

Many storms have passed by Geary Reid's way, but he has learned some important lessons so that when other storms approach him, he goes into his reservoir and applies what he knows. If many persons remain calm and walk away from problems, they will make the heart of Geary Reid glad. While there will always be problems, Reid thinks that many persons need to be quiet, think carefully, and then act. Those who are quick to act may only hurt themselves and others. So, let's stop hurting others and see many more persons having enjoyable lives.